Music Lesson

∞

Kristen Staby Rembold

FUTURECYCLE PRESS

www.futurecycle.org

Cover artwork, a section from "The Terrace at Saint-Germain, Spring" by Alfred Sisley; author photo by Christopher M. Rembold; cover and interior book design by Diane Kistner; Adobe Garamond text and titling

Library of Congress Control Number: 2018958545

Published by FutureCycle Press
Athens, Georgia, USA

ISBN 978-1-942371-64-9

To K & I, who schooled my heart

Contents

V. Picture from the Group of Seven

I. Terrain

Terrain

1.

All I see are stones, stacked stones,
when I close my eyes that evening afterward,

>   as in my youth I worked a crop—say, strawberries—
>   and spent the night, behind my lids, picking them again.

I see myself turning each rock so it nestles
closer to its neighbors, so it becomes integral to the whole,

>   as I visualized the shadow under the cutwork leaves
>   and the paler stems where the prize lay hidden.

I am learning the heft of each rock texture,
each one's hardness in respect to the other,

>   as I once looked out for the kiss of a rotted berry
>   on matted straw, mold's bloom that corrupts entire basketsful.

Why should this not seem a labor of love, this marriage
of angles, this fitting of two thicknesses to one?

>   Back then, I didn't want to dream the berries.
>   That work wasn't a labor of love, so I claimed, but only for the money.

How the tables turn. What started out as random,
whim or affinity, an accidental meeting, is what one builds upon.

2.

    Yet recall the morning, dressed in layers against morning's coolness,
    the feel of T-shirt, of flannel, of denim, frayed edge soaking up the dew;

recall this morning, in early spring, our middle-aged selves
bent over a gash in bare earth we endeavor to fill,

    when we fanned out, each with a row to work and, together,
    a field to cover, in harness with our neighbor,

to delve into this terrain with all its faults and fissures,
its richnesses we've come to know,

    with our fellow harvesters, including our sisters and brothers,
    friends and companions to whom we were accountable,

and though I hadn't wished for this life to be so circumscribed,
and though I felt myself larger,

    there was a unity as we labored together,
    our work took on a shape visible from a long distance.

3.

But we progress by the square foot,
by the click of rocks as we fit them in the puzzle,

    by the row-foot, and by the basket,
    scooting or squatting along the straw path,

and pause to reinforce, with grit and gravel, every section
and smooth the surface, rough our hands,

    staining our fingertips, tasting sand.
    Straw bit skin; the fragrance gathered.

We were always seeming to bow
or seeming to kneel.

4.

      I feel now, as I didn't then,
      there is a beauty in humility

and there is a mystery in the closest things,
a cavity we fathom by the inward-rushing gravel,

      that moment of a seed's germination,
      its urge to push forward, its reason or its lack,

the holy silences that abide
between two souls,

      the dark-faced migrant I glimpsed in barn's shadow
      when he whistled to his fellow,

what is held back,
what goes unsaid.

5.

      We rode out in a blue-cab farm truck,
      legs dangling from the back,

covered from the sun. We hadn't argued yet.
Can it be said, from this great distance,

      we were glad in each other's company, even under the watch
      of the farmer, with her gold tooth and bandana,

we were glad to apply our efforts,
stripping off layers as the day ripened,

      and, though we relished the times when the farmer turned her back,
      we carried out flats brimful with berries,

and sometimes the rocks settled into place
as if there were no other place so perfect.

II. Love Note

Love Note

See, the milkweed pod you left
on the wooden table for a souvenir
is just coming open,
its gnarled and warty husk
sculptural as if you'd taken your chisel to it
after the rough hewing was done.
No scent to it at all,
not the barest remembrance of the day
we first came upon it,
that day nearing the cusp of summer
and its blooms perfuming the whole
of the mountain meadow.
By the time we returned it was Indian summer,
the annuals nearing their demise. Who knows
how many beautiful fall days there'll be?
The husk reminds me of a cradle,
but our days of bearing are over.
Now I see how the thing was carved, measured, judged.
I touch the silk that will bear away the seed.

Daylight Savings

Early dusk, and fog rises to fill the hollows,
terrain flattens under headlamps,
becomes finite, and the infinite
becomes infinite. We make a path,

light by isolated light, to our home,
to this kitchen where dinner warms,
the house vast around us,
our faces lanterns to each other.

Birds and Bees

Though I thought they weren't ready, my confident friend,
the other gardener, thought they were,
and she was right; when we cut the spent stems,
the seed pods burst, scattering radiantly,
even before I gave each stem a quick, sharp blow.

Distinctly, I felt pellets, whether or not I was their intended,
and laughed when they stuck to my sweat, stuck in my little creases,
at such cheek, at such persistence!
Shy as I am, no casual observer would guess
I'd dare broadcast myself abroad so shamelessly.

But, once stuck, I'd be
just like those seeds that adhered to my skin all day,
little sunspots, little ink dots, travelers
I'd meant to brush loose, but not until I was in shade,
which they prefer: the flickering, the filtered light.

I know what they mean—I love it, too,
the quiet, the whispering, the susurrus,
the world as seen through curtains. Showering, I found a few
and, afterward, in bed, no doubt from my tousled
hair, my husband found one, too.

Below Zero

To a cougar's eye, I was told,
the pumping of a skier's arms
and kicking stride

look like the flailing
of a wounded animal.
Vulnerable

that next day skiing,
after I'd herringboned uphill,
lagging behind,

I couldn't keep
from staring
up into snow-laden branches

to detect a flicker, or the split pupil
of an attentive eye,
wondering

what purpose I had,
whether I was of use,
and what was my worth,

given I was so often last
or off to the side,
woolgathering.

My attention
narrowed on spruce fingers
that resembled cat's toes

with needles like claws
sheathed under snow,
thumb-shaped buds

like a cat's
vestigial paws.
I laughed to realize

how ardent
I am, how in love
with this world. Then the cold

began to prick. I listened
for my breath to punctuate
the quiet.

Mary, Why Are You Weeping?

1.

In my garden, peony buds reach,
tight-fisted, above the greenery.
A bird sings from an upper branch—

loud, impassioned—then changes his perch,
then tries again. No answer.
Inside, the phone rings

while I hesitate, my dread like the darkness
at the bottom of the thicket,
a darkness so deep, nothing grows in it.

But it's good news, not bad:
the birth of my brother's infant,
opening a motionless space within.

2.

All that buds, grows, swells,
how will it culminate?
Not everything is burgeoning—

not my father, bent,
leaning on furniture, gray-faced, panting,
who says, with a grimace, *isn't it great*

to be alive? and one can't tell:
is he cursing or blessing?
My mind escapes to the garden,

to the bird I tried to glimpse
while it was singing,
its body almost hollow,

a cavern like this one in me,
wild and holy,
suited for bleakness or devotion.

3.

Listen: finally
the bird is answered; a faint, lovely
refrain from another tree

widens into reply. Sweet assent,
just as we imagine in our dreams,
that chamber blossoming

into resonance, into singing,
just as, when I call, my father
after a gasped breath

responds with pleased surprise
and calls me by my childhood name,
which swells within me,

so what was shrill and steep
becomes sonorous and deep
in that moment of receiving.

Meditation in July

Now is a good time to think of slowness:
of dappled shadows, of wind
barely tickling the leaves; the beaten

dirt path and luminous dark stones;
the splash when the first drops of rain
strike earth and slick green vegetation;

the tugging sound, like a nursing child,
of moisture being sucked deep down into soil,
and the silence afterward.

Contemplation is more elusive now,
scarce as the old radio voices, scarce
as the dusking and dawning sounds

of the small farms you used to find everywhere—
a lost image like dust meandering after a car
on a dirt road just before it disappears

among the grains and grasses—
but the need for it still rubs like a pebble
in your shoe.

And when, in the rounds of daily life,
quietude finds you, its deliciousness is dizzying
and rare, like the sun-warmed fruit of the season.

Permit Area Only

Those boxed-in
swimming squares
are enigmas in the wilderness,
especially empty afternoons,
their rope-strung necklaces
of floats tattered, forlorn;
the lifeguard chair,
martial whistle hovering over
desert of sand, beyond
the demarcations set
for deep and shallow,
the raft afloat on barrels,
its ladder the far
limitation of summer.

Travel, Risk, Beauty

On the eve of my sister's cancer surgery,
we stayed up late to watch a movie
in which English retirees were seduced

into staying in a gorgeous, dilapidated Indian hotel;
and in the dream of mine that followed,
I persuaded you, beloved husband, not to embark

the multistoried wooden ship where, up on one of many decks,
while the female captain wasn't looking, I found you—
just curious, you said—and seized you back

from what seemed to me an ill-fated trip,
the boat about to depart into a storm from a dock
overhung with glossy-leaved, poisonous holly.

Berries of gold and scarlet, banners,
archways, portals, storm clouds, vivid skies,
glorious, oversaturated textiles with emblems of mandalas—

how strange, then, to awaken to ordinary morning,
chilly for summer, a polar bear morning in which you and I
feel our vitality, thrashing out swimming pool laps,

a day when windows are hoisted
and a breeze conveys the sharp scent
of toast I'd burnt in another room.

Even now, steam must be rising from the water
on faraway lakes, the lakes of childhood summer camps
to which my sister and I went,

where one must be brave and hold one's breath
as water rushes over one's sealed nose and lips
and one goes under.

Great Lakes

Someone said "whitecap" on the radio
and the word unfurled a sail within me,
a space, a snag.

Sometimes the whitecaps were nothing, kite-flying weather.
No small-craft warnings, no real danger.
Days to swim and swim.

In middle age, I drive daily
over this slow, brown, Southern river,
unaware of my longing until it's pronounced

and whitecaps appear to me, frothing and dangerous,
to threaten summer afternoon, put it to ruin,
dash it with their *own* beauty.

Six Lines

for Marnie

I don't know if we can bring her back,
I imagine them saying as rescuers are bending
over me—oh, despairing me—this rainy evening.
I drive into a dark so black and full of hazards, unseen
crosswalks, sudden flashes, I must hang on to the thought,
like a laundry line, that you said you'd be waiting.

∞

There's another kingdom beyond the wood fringe and fences
along the country road we drive past midnight
between our friend's home and our own,
perhaps too full of bonhomie to see
pale bodies lit by moonlight or lamplight
leaping across the starlit fields.

∞

When I speak of them at a dinner party,
my grandfather, grandmother, and great aunt
rouse themselves and reassume the shape of their clothes,
surprising me—how ever ready they stay to counsel or praise,
to serve a drink, to comment on a book, and my grandmother's hands
fly upward when she cries *Krissy's here!* as if she's still delighted.

∞

We can't revisit each place.
Some are closed off from us forever.
But from this park bench, we can see across the water
and spot the blue canoe,
the rocks where we sunbathed behind our first house,
a place we couldn't own but loved.

∞

Walking back from a yoga session
on a clear night, with stars in sharp focus,
I recognize Orion, winter hunter, by his diamond-studded belt,
then the pole star and, if I squint, the tight cluster
of the Pleiades, the seven sisters: this momentary
sense of the infinite, solitude's pleasure.

Twin Beds

in this old European inn, a room
overlooking a courtyard; a little sad

how boxed in they are, no room
for overhanging limbs; and how they creak,

like the beds of our childhoods! Something
blessed about them, too, and the flocked draperies,

the little horns of dried flowers. Even sex
must be chaste, quick, missionary.

It's Christmas in the courtyard—a nativity,
the mother's face lit, a strawed-in manger,

angels, the shepherds adoring. Who can sleep,
even once the light is out? So we lie awake,

telling unguarded thoughts,
the inn's walls sloping around us,

no shiver as body slides against body—how easily
I've learned to surrender

to that mingled unconscious. I wake to hear
a sheet of snow slip on the roof—like luxurious fabric—

and then it stops. Middle of the night.
Pine boughs, flying snow, white blazes across sky.

I, the only witness.

III. Music Lesson

Music Lesson

We stood in a clearing, her teacher and I,
while my daughter played,
floating sound out the window, over the meadow,
the violin ascending, the trees outside

stepping forward, crowding in on meadow grass,
casting the first shadow, one moment
too beautiful to look upon, with hues
that contradicted the idea of a meadow,

all the cool colors, all the lilac,
the violin's timbre while the phrase
was still aloft making it difficult
to draw breath, and dusk holding back

keeping visible the gleam, the delineated
edges of leaves, the jewel-like seed.
Brahms, in order to console himself,
wrote about the meadow grasses; he wrote

about tears seeding the wheat and the glory of man
being like the flowers of the field.
Though we loved her so,
we couldn't have stopped her

from finding out sorrow
any more than we could keep the trees
from swallowing the grasses
and the grasses from sinking into darkness.

Summer of the Cardinals

I hear the female, perched on a patio chair, singing,
after my daughter's last summer home
that began with the cardinal pair
shuttling back and forth,
knitting their nest.

Chicks peeped in the trellis
as the rose budded. A squirrel
lurked on the fringe,
about to turn bland sweetness
into something fraught. Roused
by the parents' racket, I shooed him away,
too late—only one nestling survived.

My daughter was enamored with this
awkward chick, who, toadlike, with wide
toad mouth, shrilled and shrilled,
giving his perch away, making himself
vulnerable to every enemy.
He flapped and swooped, conspicuous
and comic, across our backyard,
accompanied by his straight-man, red-suited father,
who was a worrier and had cause to be.

The youth grew a tuft,
became the color of a house finch
with his first dusty red feathers,
fell once each from the birdbath
and the feeder. We saw him less frequently,
gliding to the table or a branch,
almost—not quite—missing.

He grew redder, smoother, less visible,
then disappeared, and the only way
to distinguish him from other birds of the brush
was his insistent piping.

Now the mother I'd overlooked
reappears and sings her song.
I've left the door of my study
open to the cooler weather, to the sounds
of a crescendo, fading.

What Did the Vietnam War Mean to Me?

After the warm, still air of the capitol city,
after the memorial, we crack the car window,
our daughter's boyfriend hands us a CD,
and the music of Dylan, so long unheard, wakes us again.

Were I to say I came from a rural county,
with its rural roads and exoduses on hunting days,
where we were raised to be useful, and we could
calculate and we could troubleshoot,

would you see where this is leading?
We didn't know what to make of Dylan.
Whether we chose to be hawks or doves,
each way led to betrayal.

I don't know how love could have prevented
the long argument concerning Abraham and Isaac
that still leaves us red-faced, sputtering,
even though it is, by now, theoretical,

between fathers who were willing to send sons
and those sons who might obediently have gone.
Fathers who yell, "the Kent State massacre
wouldn't have happened if the students

hadn't been the aggressors,"
so we yell, "they had flowers!"
For we had wanted to love,
we had wanted the world to return our kisses.

So many Dylan songs turned out to be
about an inability to love,
not only war, but something more personal,
a lack within, that was what we couldn't understand,

a self-regard, a callowness that prevented
an offering of one's self, which is what we'd had to offer,
never mind how like the world it was
to take advantage of our aptitude.

The breeze blows in, my breath comes quicker,
and I feel more youthful in this different skin.
Then I realize the music isn't sirens
anymore; it's just music.

My Dream Is His Life's Museum

Why do my dreams keep vigil,
following my husband's father down corridors
and stairwells, past oak files,
objects on a wooden shelf:
photos from the turn of the nineteenth century
(not strangers, for he has acquainted me
with them; he is their reliquary),
brash two-toned ads in frames,
orange of hazard symbols,
the strange iconography of that age,
a book with chiseled type and a hero
blazing his way across the spine.

I'm awakened in this century
by a noise like ball bearings
outside, on the street below,
rolling and picking up speed,
then I drift back to sleep:
another room, a veiled argument
disagreeing with my politics,
with my disrespect for the government,
though I'm not sorry. Both his wives
wait on him. The one who died
serves with downcast eyes.

She would have hated the idea
of a second wife and hated
each injustice life perpetuated,
and, much as I've suffered at her hands,
I'm upset for her sake. But only in the dream,
not in this life, lying beside their son, wound
in sheets—three, four, five a.m.—
hours past revelry,

hours of vigil for patients in pain's bed,
and for lonely wakefulness,
quiet hours and long.

Could the first bird
of this world call and comfort me?

Question from Beethoven's Choral Symphony

The question I never dared ask my mother,
the question for which I never found words,

was, What if that reverberating *no*
were the first and last sound Beethoven ever heard,

the rumble of the bass line when the treble
winds and brass raised a fanfare like a banner

and later, even, when the fanfare reentered
humbly, as hymn, and the lower strings grumbled

their refusal? All the music I knew then
came from my mother's record collection,

albums she kept in a cabinet
under the category of things she loved,

gotten out on rare occasions:
Van Cliburn, for example, in black and white,

hands poised to pound into Rachmaninoff,
and behind his hands—wasn't there?—a shadow.

I liked to search her face for its reflection
the way a child's eyes

seek in their devotion. What did I know then?
Listening to Beethoven,

I wanted the clouds to open.
I didn't want the people Schiller says are damned

to stay damned; what of the unloved
child, the uninvited? Schiller says

come, whoever has created
an abiding friendship, or has won

a true and loving wife, join in praise;
all others must creep tearfully away.

Kyrie, Forty Years After the Riots

What am I doing in this neighborhood,
apartment hunting with my daughter,
here where the trees are staked, provisional,

bleached by chinks of light that shine
in the gaps between buildings, though more
than a generation has passed?

From blocks away I can hear the sound
of whoops and screams,
a distant roar like trees the wind is lofting.

The stifling heat, though it is only May,
reminds me nostalgically of summer
with the crescendo of a roller coaster

coming from a building on the corner,
the All Souls' Gospel Church, an ordinary
flat-roofed building except for its pulsating,

except for the fact that I can't
see inside, though who am I to see?
Two deacons guard the door, the windows secured

to protect the many, many souls
who have risen and have coalesced above their exposed
and visceral selves; they heave and emanate

something unintelligible and strange
behind folding metal screens that open out into diamonds,
a type of screen I've only seen in poor neighborhoods, with piercings

I peer into like the diamonds in the windows of confessionals—
but those are smaller and harder,
carved in wood or punched from metal.

Insomnia

What keeps our bodies,
our blood coursing—
a maddening din, like midsummer
night insects, their pitched questions?

They blink or vibrate
two dumb syllables: *alive, alive.*
The circuits, the network, this web
of connections within our own body:

the map of this skin, this brain
teeming, no matter if you ask
to what purpose
or beseech *be still.*

Even in this familiar, unfathomable acre,
darkness pulsates—across my room,
beneath my cool skin,
uncharted as space or ocean's bottom,

evidence of worlds within worlds.
I lie alone, but not alone,
accompanied by that pulse
that rules until it chooses *peace, sleep.*

On Hearing Elgar's *Pomp and Circumstance*

No more bare trim, peeling
lead-based paint, no unsafe neighborhoods
or walking out-of-doors in all weather
or talking through the night.
A few sticks of furniture buy respectability;
after that, we're afraid to give offense.

Sometimes, even now, the feeling reenters
like a door opening onto a mirror,
and we stand startled
by the force of what we were.
We were the leading edge.
We answered only to passion's
uncompromising reason,
love, love, making all else
irrelevant, all except the coursing
of our blood.

That day, I remember you cast
a look of mirth over one shoulder
because such seriousness
begged for levity
to disguise that our hearts
entered gravely into this
pageant of life.

Autumnal Equinox

to the memory of our year in Wales

This turbulent time of year,
the smooth water that would have floated you
to the further shore
turns inward upon itself, ruffled
by disturbances you wouldn't have guessed.

No sign yet on land, not the buff-colored
grasses stirring on the clifftop, nor blackberries
plucked poignant and sweet, nor the bright painted
doors of the village, not even orange leaves
blown across the tannin darkness of the pond.

But old wives' tales warn of unsettled weather.
People returning early to their houses
snap on lights while cooking dinner.
The ten-to-six shipping news forecasts gales,
calls the seas by name.

If your ship is out to sea, you may wake
in darkness, not knowing with any certainty
where you may be—in the belly of the beast?—
your berth pitching along with each swell, forcing you
to call out for whatever god you worship, after all.

Summer Afternoon

Summer afternoon, summer afternoon;
to me those have always been the two most
beautiful words in the English language. —Henry James

One June day, after attending a wedding,
we are driving down a country road

past banks starred with daylilies
on our way to another party,

feeling married and enclosed
as rain flecks our windows,

lashing the car, the road, the grasses,
the bright and hot transformed

into a blue-green, swaying, seaweedy crossing,
the grasses and lilies bearing down,

and we immerse ourselves, too, like swimmers
headed across a body of water

on a summer's passage
to the next island or point across the bay,

hoping our stamina will not fail.
Lately, one or the other of us has been lagging,

as if we suffer from the same anomaly—
a hole in the heart—

that brought on the stroke
from which our daughter now haltingly recovers.

We step out into moisture dripping from trees
as on long-ago vacations up in Canada or New Hampshire

when I was a child or we had children,
when this sort of start

boded how the whole day would be—
not very summery.

But we insisted on it being summer,
and so it was.

Mystery

World, once taken for granted
before a flash, infarction, the one-sided
grimace, the unfinished

gesture if you could raise
your arm, move
your tongue—

rushed by ambulance,
scanned, infused,
implored, because you are loved,

oh, come back to us!
Your lips formed the words
of a meaningless sentence.

You lost the better part of a year
in your slow climb back
some called miraculous,

but what of the force revealed
that wants destruction,
or is indifferent, or has no power...?

World, once taken for granted, streams past
particolored, sometimes too loud;
it must be handled carefully.

Your first outing into the city,
you breathe it in deeply
with reverence and joy.

You stroll, you hold hands,
you see a play, and afterwards
you discuss it brilliantly.

You nod in the train on your way back
because you're tired, because
you know you can't have it all,

because knowing what you can have,
but might not, you're satisfied.
But someone, someone outside,

standing on a bridge,
about to take a leap onto the tracks,
thinks otherwise.

Hard Frost

Past midnight, dropping me off from the airport
at our childhood home, my sister said, "Look, you can see
it's frosting now." Outside the half-empty
house, when I wake, the frost is prodigious:
leaves frosted all the way up the stems, even the dissected
leaves of the Japanese maple and the blue-green needled
foliage of evergreens, frosted berries, silvered shades
of rose, mahogany, burgundy and bronze,
and finally of the silvered grass. My parents,
still sleeping, one home, one at the hospital,
will puzzle at my arrival. Below this window,
pale frozen rosebuds nod over
the downturned head of a concrete angel,
her ankles crossed, a book on her lap,
who will never turn a page,
who sits upon her pedestal forever.

What, Exactly, Is This Cold?

Is it snow or frost, and what comprises sadness?
I put my finger to the wind, which, if it answers,
answers in another tongue,
and when I look for something written down,
I see the windows have been etched, and the ground.

As I walk, the only moving things I see
are robins harvesting a crabapple tree.
The widower at his window
will be waiting a long while. Nor can we friends meet
and brush cheeks, pat shoulders, share compliments or sympathy.

Mailboxes stand with their flags frozen up.
Driveways form slippery dark ribbons and, along the road,
ice crystals chase each other in a circle, they whirl
while my mind obliges, plays Tchaikovsky
softly, so I hear each key.

IV. Long Ago

Long Ago

They come to a stop
at a distant bay, cut
the motor, rock and bob
in the wave-chop,
drifting from shore,

its lichened rocks,
grassed slope, shuttered
splattered house and silent bell.
A centeredness,
a bowing forward.

She and her father,
bobbins open,
flick to cast, line glinting
as it unspools, crosses over,
back, faster

than fish
leaping, than mind's
eye, away and away,
then sinks in place.
She keeps asking,

begging,
when they finish, not to go
straight home
but farther,
to the rocky ledge,

rocks striped red
and flecked with mica
like pictures she's seen of Jupiter
at school, tapped
by the rubber-tipped pointer.

There, before
the aster fringe
and nursery of evergreens,
if you climb the rock
you can find the edge

where rock meets soil,
where flints and shards
sparkle in the dust.
That was what
she'd wanted.

But she never shakes the fear
that, when she returns,
islands will seem other worlds,
channels will seem other seas,
so she'll be lost

and fail to spot
the channel leading to the harbor,
just as she's never been able
to locate empty seats in a crowded room
or a child

in a throng,
suddenly aware
of the cold, wishing for
the haven of familiar
hands and faces,

for the rough-
textured terry towel
used to rub
someone awake
or alive.

Aurora Borealis

Somewhere near, along the ridgetops,
the northern lights have been radiantly shining,
but she lives here below, in this bowl of light.
She hasn't seen them since she was a child,
when they were pointed out to her:
"Look North, toward Canada."
Whose voice, she cannot say;
it was spoken in the voice of a deity.

She imagines she can remember, too,
that otherworldly hiss and howl, the distance
between earth and sun charged,
waves of strange vibrations.
She thinks of the playing of a saw
as she heard it on the radio,
but the memory may have been no more
than a child's wonder at the vastness of night sky,
the wide sweep of winter wind.

The Year My Father Was Born

In 1933, the breadline
snaked along
pavement and facade,
the hunger that
was always there
dredged up from dream
or nightmare:
cool daylight
straining through
coal dust
they'd become
accustomed to,
men to the shovel,
women
to the washcloth
and bucket,
and yet—
could
they be?—
grateful
to labor,
especially
the many
immigrants
and immigrants'
children
who'd fled
from an even more
dread dream.
December shone
its short, slant light
on these weary-
shouldered

drab-coated
supplicants,
on trainyard
laborer and office
boy alike,
making of these
poor materials
a tapestry,
because one of the sun's
gifts is shadow.
The children
born that year
were always hungry
and labored
all they could,
because, otherwise,
how would they
be worthy?

Missing

in memory of the Rev. Scott Jones

A crowded store, I see you in line.
You look so kind. You smile slightly
and step aside. Your hooded eyes are enigmatic.

The line surges and you draw your wallet.
Dead men have wallets? I thought
they gave them up, along with their keys
and coins. I've thought of you, dispersed.

The jangle of change
as you stand musing makes me know
it *is* you—you, containing your secret
thoughts forevermore.

Fiftieth Anniversary of the Kennedy Parade

People speak of how many presidents they've seen
or who was president when they were born.
Eisenhower was mine, and I was there on October 12, 1962

in Buffalo, N.Y. when Kennedy's parade passed by, my father
holding me on his shoulders above the vast crowd and boulevard
where each face was a fleck no larger than a grain of a newspaper photo,

nor could I make them out as faces, and I realized
that we were flecks, too; moreover, the light and breeze
that had set off a restless flickering of flags in all directions

also touched on me so I felt the first sting
of who knows what it was—
a seed, a speck, some grit aloft in the wind,

the seed of my resistance, a wayward seed,
hard and resolute as a kernel of wheat,
key to my difference and my loneliness,

a loneliness I had already felt—and was astonished
though that didn't keep me from clinging
harder to my father with my hands and knees,

such was his nature and such was mine. Nor did I escape—I felt—
the current passing through the crowd, excitement for Dad,
a shiver for me, when President Kennedy's car whisked by.

The Shortest Day

As I knelt
in a chair by the window,
gray sky turned inside-out to flannel
and stars, as they appeared,
winked to ice crystals,
a soft sifting

falling
in silence. Was this
all the day there was?
I called to my mother for the time.
Not yet four? A harrowing
I still can feel.

But I willed something more
to appear, and streetlight
swelled to star,
blue deepened
and became fleecy
as the inside of my sleeve.

Half Acre

When she was a girl, there was a season
she liked to walk with the moon-faced boy
from down the street through the field

filled with grasses whispering and wildflowers
tangled and flared, insect clicks,
and sometimes a flickering mouse or snake

on its own errand. "What are you doing?"
faint parental voices called, and the temptation
was not to answer, if answering meant

to step back into obedience.
Yet, it was innocent—
he would take her hand

as he spoke, to show her something,
and fix her with his eyes,
knowing that she shared his amazement

whenever a puff of breeze lofted leaves
and tugged at Indian paintbrush
or when a killdeer ran along

foraging in midday heat.
That half acre, like the boy,
was quiet, or it raged.

Come each fall, his father torched
the field, and it would blaze
to emptiness, only to refill itself again.

She remembered this long after she'd changed
and the gentle boy who'd loved her
had grown so nobody could manage him.

Memorial Day Clambake, 1970

A country girl, well-practiced,
used to chores and tasks,
huddles with the other adolescents
in the still-cool morning,
setting up the tinder and the kindling,

sheltering the fire like a nest
so it will flame and catch
against a field of gray and brown and green,
against a sky, overcast,
against familiar elements,

stone and flesh, dooryard and farmyard,
fanning that rainbow of flame—
life, unbridled, as she imagines,
its roar distant and deafening,
all-engulfing—

tending the blaze
of the rebellious heart she holds
unsuspected,
the rift between
this landscape and herself.

She feeds the flames,
breathes on them as God breathed
life into man, building
a shrine for fire
where the flames dance like Shiva's

four hands—flicker, shiver,
spark—all the sinuous
arms, all the precious
gold and bangles,
so the flames rage

against the four square
cabin walls,
and even the tepee wails
Who will step forward?
Who will be called?

Once tindered, the spark
can't be controlled,
catches the shirt of the girl
who stood too close,
who didn't mean to be

speaking in tongues,
casting a woeful
look over her shoulder, as if she
only now could see what's coming,
like those immolating

monks regarding their robes
on the temple steps,
some ill wind
she didn't guess,
until her mother comes crying

the girl's name
in incantation,
running, amazing her
with her body, her outstretched
arms.

Long Cry After Reading *The Mill on the Floss*

1.

She keeps saying "Sorry, sorry, sorry"
as she poles her boat downriver,
passing relatives who line the bank—
father, mother, cousin, brother,

childhood companions—
their bootsoles sunk in the sodden
tow path. Because the river
is a moving ribbon and the sky

streams also,
she is given only a glimpse
of each as she floats past
so their figures become sentinels,

part of the landscape of water meadows,
gnarled willows and patches of wildflowers
where the eye of her affections
has extravagantly dwelled.

2.

Between the river and the tow path,
grass interposes; its yellowy green
blades flicker one by one, each light-struck
from a different angle, each

tinged a different color,
but they move as a whole
when the wind stirs,
obscuring, softening the lines

of long skirts and aprons and trousers.
She's carried past steeple and parsonage,

shops, a cottage row, all portals
particular to the life that is her own,

those dooryards filled with implements,
those low-beamed thresholds
one must bow to enter,
and, above, a cloud-smudged sky

that would send the maids and housewives of this world
running for their laundry, that would have sent her,
were she one with this world, were it not
divided in two by her fealty and hurt—

3.

a hurt that runs unstaunched
like the swollen river that flows beneath her,
smooth yet astounding in its surge,
its muscular strength and coolness,

this river that, tamed, can turn the wheel
that grinds the grain and, wild,
tears through diverters and dams
and drowns the livestock.

Is the current more to be feared or the backwater?
Submerged limbs, which at first seem flat,
lie in suspension, layer below layer
of mud-blanched leaves

that become more dimensional, deeper and darker,
the longer one looks. They won't snag her.
Already she can't remember
whether those who watched her departure

waved, or whether anyone cried or turned away.
Her movement blurred their faces
as the cool wind rippled the surface,
like shivers for what she'd done.

At February's End

It's the first warm day, tomato seeds
waiting to germinate beside the stove,
the newly emerged winged ants flying
through the kitchen, looking for their home.

> *What would it be like to be a stranger*
> *walking abroad, over hill and field and stone?*

Outside, the first harsh sun casts shadow
through a stand of trees, patterning
the ground: charcoal on silver-gray,
a contrast for hungry eyes.

I'm rolling out dough
the yellow-white of winter bark
in smooth, long strokes,
shaping my contentment.

> *If my longing could become the wind, I'd skim*
> *the blue hollow rising to the farming town*
> *where I lived.*

I don't know why I say this.
I lean close to the kitchen window
of the house we made, far south.

Wind rouses the trees, and nests
become visible in the crowns, vulnerable
as they always were, before I took notice.

Town Line Road by Bicycle, Years Later

I'm riding close
to the torn sedge at road's margin,
past wasted fields guarded by hell's dogs,

still the same
painted rocks and tire gardens,
the curve where the barn shoulders its bulk,

the cars on blocks
lying at rest, the orange
triangles of farm machinery, sumac groves

emitting their faint
green air of poison, dust
on the leaf blades, grit on the tongue.

The still air
as I enter waits for me to part it,
and when I have gone it seals closed again,

the air's suspended
before the ax falls, wood splitting
with a hollow thwack, birds on wire fences

not singing yet,
and the children who left here
years ago still gone, farmers aging;

some died,
left the porch roof sagging
without a cord of wood to rest it on.

Harvest

The crops come in order, unbidden,
from her memory—the cabbage stink
of cole crops as the spring is waning,
onions bundled in the barn,
peavines they pulled before the plow.

She knows them by heart, much as
she remembers liturgical phases: Lent,
Easter, Pentecost. The morning breeze
down the new and distant streets
where she now lives still finds her

twisting in her dreams
of that house, that bed, those sheets.
She wonders will she ever escape
the smells of dairy blowing their way,
those mornings of her mother's voice

calling up from the foot of the stairs.
She can hear, just barely,
the distant work sounds of crops
being lifted onto farm trucks,
loaded into cribs.

She used to think of them
as summer farmers, producers
of beans, tomatoes, cukes, and sweet corn.
On still days in the heat of noon,
a breeze of green confetti blew

from the green bean truck en route to the cannery.
But the green was only temporary—
soon, the bruised beans browned to chaff.
It saddened her, that wasted largesse.
(Those "fine feelings" made her mother laugh.)

So, why can't she remember
what a farmer would be doing
on this October day? Sometimes
she'd be sent to pick the fallen fruit
from beneath the shade of orchard trees

where the long, fine grass resembles baby hair
once it has been combed by the rake.
Careful, careful not to arouse the drowsy,
drunken yellow jackets and yellow-flashed hornets
lurking in the rotten fruit!

She still can smell the vinegar.
She pictures the corn, cut and shocked,
and the gaping black of open barn doors—
black against green-trimmed white,
black against cheerful red.

V. Picture from the Group of Seven

Picture from the Group of Seven

I have often stopped on the landing
to stare at this framed print
of a bountiful garden past maturity.
I would stop and think of melancholy.

But why melancholy?
Is it something about the faded hues
of mustard and olive and off-red?
Maybe it's the black outlines,

as in an etching or engraving,
but coarser and blacker,
like block printing, with channels
cut by a body leaning on a chisel—

a tool for digging
like the hoe that must lie just offstage
from the picture, waiting to turn
the composting leaves into soil.

I think I recognize this place,
or at least this frame of mind,
with the garden just past the peak of all its glory—
its heavy fruits and brilliant petals—

sometime in mid-August
before the cool of fall sets in,
the shadows and undersides becoming visible,
manifested by crosshatches and lines.

Sometime while I wasn't looking,
busy with preparations, engaged in my work,
it happened. No more than the complications
that arise in an ordinary life:

faults, illness, sadness, a child's failure to thrive.
I pause on the stairs to think of these things

and notice how dishabille has overtaken
the orderly way in the picture:

tattered foliage and striations
that had been obscured by lushness
have just begun to appear.
On the stalks of sunflowers,

first dots, then streaks,
a shocking red like blood
you wouldn't have expected
shading deeper into mahogany.

As in my life, a more worn and patient,
less believable version of myself
has learned to perform ministrations,
driving a friend to the hospital,

sharing in joy,
all the careful acts that mend an enmity.
Now I see how thrust gives way
to thickening and woodiness,

to the gnarled and curious,
the turned aside. Finally,
after all these years and flights,
I come to see the beauty.

Autumn Inventory

Leaves swirl in a whirlwind over land,
leaves skim the lake like junks in Hong Kong's harbor,
fall breezes coming in, and I, reclining
in this Adirondack chair, sleep-deprived,
still half in each element, realize I only stayed
awake last night for the sake of time alone.

I see for all those years of trying to fit myself in,
forced to ride across long nights on horseback,
thrashing through events and people of the day,
I had been in ignorance about myself.
I feel the shiver when sky becomes visible again
behind the bare-limbed walnut tree.

I feel as helpless before what is
as the solitary yellow jacket picking its way
through the leavings, confused, perhaps
disconsolate as it circles my coffee cup,
knowing something's wrong and yet persisting
in wrongheadedness. Something must change.

I must learn to love the ragged things.
I must learn to love myself.

To Old Dresses Hanging in My Closet

puffed-sleeved, princess-seamed, A-lined, mandarin-
collared, midi or mini,

to their fabrics, weaves, surfaces, patterned or figured,
with figures that often were flowers, when I was young,

to patterns that were facsimiles of myself,
cut out flat, then joined and shaped

to my body, both the same and not the same,
the familiar curves of forearm, shoulder, breast, rise of the mons,

and to the body's underpinnings, jut of the hips, the collarbone
from which the clothes were hung

whether the body beneath now swells or strains,
or the fabric drapes mysteriously over my slighter self,

for each was of an age, each I remember being
sheathed in, wrapped, bound, or caressed,

each moment hovers when called to mind, blue silk
launch parties, seersucker backyard gatherings, flocked ceremonies,

times I overcame the strange burden of being myself,
of being unsure, to be able to say *how I lived!*

to the slips and stockings that were my second skin,
to the fastenings, buttons, zippers, hooks and eyes,

and to the hands that fastened me, those who loved me,
to the ruffle of taffeta, to those I gathered in,

to the fitting rooms of grand department stores,
being driven by my mother-in-law,

who asked me what was the point of therapy
back when I was too young to know

and had to summon grace to answer,
to being the object of affection in my daughter's eyes

when a homely, button-front, flowered frock
lights her face with recognition.

I handle them reverently, these old phantoms,
these styles that can never be worn again, aged so long

trying them on is like archeology,
their styles dating them like strata date pottery.

Acknowledgments

I am grateful to the journals in which the following poems were originally published, sometimes in earlier forms:

Blueline: "Permit Area Only"
Broad River Review: "Insomnia"
Crab Orchard Review: "To Old Dresses Hanging in My Closet"
Green Mountains Review: "Love Note"
The Hopper: "Long Ago"
Iron Horse Review: "What Did the Vietnam War Mean to Me"
New Ohio Review: "Half Acre"
Red Earth Review: "At February's End"
Smartish Pace: "Terrain"
South Dakota Review: "Town Line Road by Bicycle, Years Later"
Southern Poetry Review: "Meditation in July," "Autumnal Equinox"

"Half Acre," "Love Note," "Music Lesson," and "Summer of the Cardinals" were previously published in *Leaf and Tendril* (Finishing Line Press, 2012).

I give thanks to the friends, family, and fellow writers who have offered their encouragement and suggestions, including Susan Bagby, Dan Bieker, Juliet DaLuiso, Danny Becker, Charlotte Matthews, Susan Shafarzek, and Susan Imhof of For Crying Out Loud; Charlottesville WriterHouse; Marnie Cobbs, J. C. Todd, Babo Edwards, Marianne Boruch, Maurice Manning, Joan Aleshire, Michael Collier, Martha Rhodes, Rick Barot, and countless other members of the community of Warren Wilson MFA Program for Writers; and, most of all, the dear friends and four generations of family who keep me wrapped in love, especially Chris.

About FutureCycle Press

FutureCycle Press is dedicated to publishing lasting English-language poetry books, chapbooks, and anthologies in both print-on-demand and Kindle ebook formats. Founded in 2007 by long-time partners and independent editor/publishers Diane Kistner and Robert S. King, the press incorporated as a nonprofit in 2012. A number of our editors are distinguished poets and writers in their own right, and we have been actively involved in the small press movement going back to the early seventies.

The FutureCycle Poetry Book Prize and honorarium is awarded annually for the best full-length volume of poetry we publish in a calendar year. Introduced in 2013, our Good Works projects are anthologies devoted to issues of universal significance, with all proceeds donated to a related worthy cause. Our Selected Poems series highlights contemporary poets with a substantial body of work to their credit; with this series we strive to resurrect work that has had limited distribution and is now out of print.

We are dedicated to giving all of the authors we publish the care their work deserves, making our catalog of titles the most diverse and distinguished it can be, and paying forward any earnings to fund more great books.

We've learned a few things about independent publishing over the years. We've also evolved a unique, resilient publishing model that allows us to focus mainly on vetting and preserving for posterity poetry collections of exceptional quality without becoming overwhelmed with bookkeeping and mailing, fundraising activities, or taxing editorial and production "bubbles." To find out more, come see us at www.futurecycle.org.

The FutureCycle Poetry Book Prize

All full-length volumes of poetry published by FutureCycle Press in a given calendar year are considered for the annual FutureCycle Poetry Book Prize. This allows us to consider each submission on its own merits, outside of the context of a contest. Too, the judges see the finished book, which will have benefitted from the beautiful book design and strong editorial gloss we are famous for.

The book ranked the best in judging is announced as the prize-winner in the subsequent year. There is no fixed monetary award; instead, the winning poet receives an honorarium of 20% of the total net royalties from all poetry books and chapbooks the press sold online in the year the winning book was published. The winner is also accorded the honor of being on the panel of judges for the next year's competition; all judges receive copies of all contending books to keep for their personal library.

www.ingramcontent.com/pod-product-compliance
Lightning Source LLC
Chambersburg PA
CBHW070009100426
42741CB00012B/3171